The Uncertainty Principle

The Uncertainty Principle

Roxanna Bennett

TIGHTROPE BOOKS

Tightrope Books
167 Browning Trail
Barrie, Ontario. L4N 5E7
www.tightropebooks.com

Editor: Deanna Janovski
Typography: Dawn Kresan
Author photo credit: Edward Barao

Printed and bound in Canada

We thank the Canada Council for the Arts, the Ontario Arts
Council, and the Government of Ontario through the book pub-
lishing tax credit for their support of our publishing program.

Canada Council
for the Arts
Conseil des Arts
du Canada

ONTARIO ARTS COUNCIL
CONSEIL DES ARTS DE L'ONTARIO

Ontario
Société de développement
de l'industrie des médias
de l'Ontario

Library and Archives Canada Cataloguing in Publication

Bennett, Roxanna, 1971–, author
        The uncertainty principle / Roxanna Bennett.

Poems.

ISBN 978-1-926639-77-2 (PBK.)

        I. Title.

PS8603.E55955U53 2014   C811'.6   C2014-902826-1

*For Connor Courage Bennett, of course,
and for Steve J., without whom I cannot*

and for Debra Bennett: may all your days be tens

Contents

THE DOMINANT O

So Long, Leonard

Leonard Cohen, we will never sleep together,
for I am late spring, wet earth, trees black and green,
and you are winter, fields dead beneath your weather,
starving animals molting fur, grinning and growing lean.
I won't be your footnote, a name notched on your worn belt,
a minor chord, one of the girls, Suzanne, Heather, Marianne.
You'll not be my teacher, nor know how I would have knelt
in hot hollows at your feet. You will never be my man.
I've my own frayed belt of men, mangled, notched into nothing,
too many names, a rosary of ruddy-cheeked boys, a few Gregs,
many Mikes. Long lists lost and forgotten, numbers under my skin.
On the hand-me-down turntable, you sing, while I sit quiet, cross-legged.

In Chinatown the rain beats on my back a bored tattoo.
Outside the window Venus hangs, burning brightly, slightly blue.

Jeremy

Three hours I waited for you on the museum steps,
brushing dirt from a borrowed dress, smoking
one cigarette after the next. All others had been eclipsed
by your white hair, the birthmark on your back
a map of Scotland, the sharp bones in your shoulders
where, you said, they had clipped off your wings.
Your command of paint, how colours smouldered
under your brush. That brief hush after the sting
of your words. There are spaces you have left
in the bed, in the portrait of a sick girl, retreating.
Your shadow still hangs like an atomic silhouette.
No artifacts prove we were here, and did love, briefly.

Late summer, the sun set swift, the concrete grew cold.
The bracelet on my ankle gleamed, a dull fool's gold.

Hook-up

When she passes the alley now she gives a quick glance
to the doorway's grim steel, bolts that dug into her back,
glass under heel, scrim of piss, brick, graffiti. Chance
cast a thin line into the drunk dark, quick secret heat, slack
in the system's blunt routine. Cold front cracked, mute,
she stumbles up the steps, his thick fingers slick in her jeans,
weight like an anchor while he fumbles his dick hard, brute
monotony. Simultaneously she inhabits a blank gap; between
thrust, grunt, silence transmits a spreading signal, adapts
itself to disgust, limits while lessening greed's brunt.
Later, rigging reason, what remains is the brief relief kept
souvenir, solution to the usual clamour. Skilled stunt
to sustain the sham. Call it fun what passes for distraction,
hate, or lust, hasty hunger, aphasic interlude and its transaction.

Gravity's Hook

If you weren't broke before, now there's nothing left.
When sober was a state you could relate to, you took
a soft stab at the heart, his lapels fat fistfuls, the lift
propelled his lips upward to yours, gravity's hook

undone, a state you could relate to. He took
what you gave, then refused. Seduced by argument
that propelled his lips upward to yours, gravity's hook
an earthward tug at your muscle, pulp, body's descent

what you gave, then refused. Seduced by argument,
philosophy's frantic hand-job in a scummy pub, drink
an earthward tug at your muscle, pulp. Body's descent
irresistible to the intoxicated and guilty. You link

philosophy to a frantic hand-job in a scummy pub. Drink.
If you weren't broke before, now there's nothing left
that's irresistible to the intoxicated and guilty. You link
a soft stab at the heart to his words, his rebuff, its heft.

Nom de Plume

The heart of a man is mean, shrunken, scarred
by previous tenants. Four chambers full, and not
of you. Septum thinly separates father, job, hard

artery wife, soft atrium locker-room boy. Thick clot
in the stream, rupture of soft tissue; it was like this
when you arrived. Even a trained crack shot

can't punch a hole through a gorged aorta. Subsist
on the scraps pinched from the pulmonary. Surrogate
for someone who reminds him of someone missed,

short chain back to innocence, where once on a date
he kissed a girl whose name he didn't know; the guilt
still a critical risk. What you mean here predates

you. You'll get the nom de plume, vagary, common jilt.
He wants what he sees which is not you. Hunger in
the weak chambers is for what you trigger, tilt

of blood in that first rush toward another, shock of skin,
hard thrust. Lost, but living cellular, callow lust within.

Gun Moll

He only loves you when he's drunk, halfway in
a bottle of bathtub gin, forgets to reject evidence.
Do the math, fall short of lonely, you're a has-been,
never, consort illusory. Sober keeps the pretense
of congeniality. No foul play, but overstayed inside
his story written around you, before. Would have
protected this grift, his gun moll, but it's subsided,
fixation fed. Pretend it's not related, detach
from what satiated to subsistence. He merely
sought the mystery, entertained temptation's
antidote to apathy. You're a casualty he cavalierly
stalked then discarded. At your age, desperation's
offensive. He wants to but won't, not cruel; feckless.
Fool, succumbing to the futile. Faith made you reckless.

Issha Zetsumei

What's stolen dearer than what's earned;
control disappeared with a come-on. By chance
he saw her stripped onstage, undone, burned
raw. Instantly, her lips tripped his stance,
what he had thought was his immovable mind.
At short range he fired her flippant fan mail.
Then the world zeroed. She froze in his line
of sight, flawed mirror form of a girl. Details
like career, wife, slipped like brittle straw men
through his caged fingers. What's right is not
what he desired. She incited argument,
invited dissent, reflected then severed the plot
from his own story. She made him hero, lover, liar,
quarry. Quickly. He gets one kiss. One shot and expire.

Briar Rose

Stockpiling every needle drawn
from lying eyes, each spindle,
spike, pin; can't cheat the long
con of the curse. Compelled
like a sleepwalker she'll play
with what pierces skin, scam
of the shiny spin: to be always
complete. Sweet talker's sham
refined by hundreds of hostile
royal fathers, dead mothers
releasing daughters, fertile,
guileless, to his hand. Other
loyal suitors rot in the rampart of the rose's briar,
her body delayed for the kickstart kiss of the liar.

The Robber Bridegroom

Sweetheart, the dream is not ended.
In the wood I came at last to a house,
the rooms empty, lonely, wretched,
but for a songbird and kitchen crone,

both warned me to turn back or die.
My intended, they said, was no decent
man, sweetheart. At a sound I hid behind
a cask. Two women bound in torment

tumbled through the door, a mob
of you behind them. I watched parts
of girls pile up as you cut the throb
from hearts, used teeth to tease apart

muscle from skin, flinging meat for
the old woman's boiling cauldron;
feast of no one's daughters anymore.
Gold glitter on a little finger thrown

to my feet. I caught it, token of witness.
After you savaged, swallowed bones,
slept, I slipped from slaughter's nest,
following the trail of ashes home.

Sweetheart, my dream is not ended.
This ring is evidence, all that's left
of this wedding. Begin your defence.
I won't be numbered among your dead,

bloody stains on a marriage bed.

The Mermaid's Sisters

No one can say she wasn't warned,
       trading grace for bloody footprints,
          siren song for silence. We mourned
             when she hit the shore, convinced
                we could buy her back by hacking
                         off the ribbons of our hair;
                   the gift is always sacrifice. She, lacking
                voice or reason, gave short shrift
          to our pleas, threats, no sibling
    could compare to the chance
    glance of a stranger. The King,
          our father, ordered oceans
                         to flood the world of man.

                                        She waved goodbye
until she drowned, parade boats of princes floating overhead.
       She should have kept distant, detected danger,

                                 left him for dead.

Hummingbird Heart

She wants to brand his pen name on her hidden skin,
undress him with her teeth, tongue her way
through the arc of his throat but he's forbidden;
she can't mark him for her own, pin him down, lay
claim, play coy. Powerless to expose, possess, she
can't withstand her own need. Obsessed, shown
her greed, grinding slowly, soaked, against his knee;
allows him to command, provoke, evoke low moan,
grip her hips, slip in a merciless kiss, feed her what
she knows will destroy her. All she can't live with.
Under his hands she's mute, thrall to torment, hot
shocks shoot through her hummingbird heart, frantic,
hungry. Shy of sudden pursuit, unnerving surrender,
she submits to the terminal love of a stranger.

Petechia

Restraint left delicate disfigurement, imprint
of a single finger, cruel in pallor, dying under
unseen hands. Faint stain lingers in skin,
what remains. Broken capillaries seep, surround
tissue, unhurried darkening from livid red, vivid
blue, smear of lantern green. Nerve endings
detect increased severity of pressure, perceived
as pain. Hidden rosette meagre reminder, sting
of a kiss so violent it altered cells. Cherish grief's
perishing blemish, commit to sustain explainable
damage. Collude to contain what can't quit, brief
clandestine compulsions, obsession unobtainable.

Smaller contusions resolve rapidly when reabsorbed, subside into the body.
But larger, deeper ones sometimes harden, won't heal. There is no remedy.

The Bottle Genie

I'm the empty room you fill with all your damaged objects,
what you've dragged behind you expecting future perfect.

I'm the parked white van ageing by the curb all summer
that you're about to drive into the river. A connoisseur

of you. I'm the creature you'll take fresh organs from when
yours atrophy, wither. Your guarantee. Half clone, half twin,

all mirror. I'm your well artesian, Delphic oracular, murmur
in your empty ear, place you draw your meanest words. Liquor

pressed to your chest, fluid, slick and rapid, spill me from
your lips to what's below. I'm the third in your threesome,

every cum-covered porn star you've ever jacked off to. Let
you do what you can't admit you need. I'm an exotic pet,

plucked, docile, but ferocious when you want me to be.
I'm the pit you'll bury me in when you're done with me.

I'm the bottle genie you shrink, contain to do as you command,
hot hard little minx you can restrain. Unlike her, I understand.

I'm what you push your fists into when dailiness makes you
homicidal, the number you dial when you're suicidal, subdue

your hunger, eat the rage you carry. I'm pliant, stay where
you put me. Key to the cage you've married, electric chair.

I'm what quells the terror, haunts rivals, scorns your adversaries.
I'm the shoebox of your secrets, vacant lot where you hide the bodies,

your underscore. I'm your backdrop, prop. I'm your getaway, bail
bond, underbelly. I'm your soundtrack, 12 on the Beaufort scale.

I'm the empty window panes in a scissored newspaper, finger
of air beneath the door. I'm the cold chisel killing the torch singer,

the alembic that distills you to vapour. I'm what analyzes your
labelled slides, you in my eyes, magnified. I'm your cellar door.

I'm faithful, fervid, your biggest fan, ardent audience, assistant
to your magician's trick. Gracious, vicious, voice what you think.

I'm the night bell you ring at the roadside motel. I'm the boxcar
you ride to vagabond beyond the banal bloat. I'm your bell jar,

black flag, shock absorber, dog tag. I'm the war you wage against
the grind that murders you. I'm your game plan, first mate.

I'm who you punish with a blindside. I'm the girl you turn
toward the tree at night, hiked skirt, slide inside. I'm the burned

down town of your childhood. I'm the twister you glimpsed
peripherally from the back seat of every forced fun family trip.

I'm the slit to sink your brittle spall, your first-class fluffer.
I'm everything you've wished for. You're everything I suffer.

Inamorata

If it's love you covet don't forget what you paid
for. Baby, I'll pick your bones, nest inside
the cracked cage of your ribs. Suck your sticky
misery, bruised belly, swell your bit lips. Your
suffering my succour, Sugar. Let's explore how much
you can endure. Confide in me, Honey, let me tie you
down, ride you sore. Deplore the bad luck desire's
accident loosed into your bed. Sweetie, you asked for
this when you saw me from a distance, sketched a script
with me, miscast, as the last chance you had for diversion.
A glance let you think yourself man enough to master
the trick of me. Don't take it personally when I undo you.
I'm the hilt end of the knife. Unstitch what hitches you
to your known world, fling you free. It's what you get for
begging me to wade through the wreckage of your life.

November

A ring is a thin thing to guard against
the quick sting of the first awkward
trembling touch, or the stain rain
leaves on pavement, pools of dark
beneath the playground. Autumn,
he's wearing that coat again,
his hair longer, struck dumb
by his eyes. She should. It's late.
"Hurricanes," the cabbie said.
"We've all got to watch out for
natural disasters." A new dread
of goodness, leaning by his door.
Amber haloes the halogens, blue
blur of the cold road. Scarlet
maples flame brief against the black.
The back seat—home.

Uprising

He's on the seawall fixed between
son, wife and misery. Vancouver fences
him in with its junkies, memories,
strung-out ferry rides—
in Stanley Park he's lost
in the verdant uprising

of green. She's in Toronto, an uprising
of smokestacks, skyscrapers, between
points on a subway map, lost.
Limits of middle age fence
her in, a dozen lives ride
on her decisions. Memories,

raw beauty of teenage selves, memories,
youth that saw thoughtless uprising,
riots, tumult and blankly rode
out the result. Now the story between
them: unseen spies fenced
in by duty, debt. Art shelved, lost

opportunities, moments. Heart lost
to the lure of lying memories.
Resentment, threat of upset fences
in the possibility of an uprising.

Apart, the fragile disguises between
them falter in a time machine ride

to places they inhabited, subway rides,
back alleys, bars, ghosts of lost
geography hidden between
circumstance and memories.
Chances are the heart's uprising
will leave grief, debris, fractured fences,

agony. Degrees of disappointment fence
with increments of hope, outcome rides
on replacement actors. Fact is, uprising
is unlikely. Endless hours lost
to futile schemes and intrigue. Memory
represses the obsession. Between
confessions fixed in illicit tenderness and lost
promise rides moral sense, subdued memories
of an aborted uprising, the thwarted love between.

Break Up

Or hash it out with hang-ups, callbacks, all-caps
emails. Post the extra keys and turn the paintings
to the walls. Burn the evidence. Divide albums,
books, sift through the wreckage. Mine, yours,
mine, mine, mine. Assess the damage.
Find a home for the dog. Unknot the bed
sheets and dig deep in the closet. Separate
the silverware, the knives from the knives.
Shrink back as you walk by. Keep to
the doorways. Finger the ring your
coffee cup left on the dining table,
the spoon you licked tilted at a guilty angle.
White daisies wilted in a square glass jar.
Things, all things, only mean when
we see. It's for the best. Change your
address. Change your name. Store what
you can't carry. Chuck the rest.

Another Motive for Metaphor

(After Wallace Stevens's *A Motive for Metaphor*)

You like it under the bridge in summer
because everything is half-drunk,
the wind limps beneath the trestle,
a crippled echolaliac.

In this way, you were happy in winter
with the sharp edge of white, the half melt,
the strict blue, the geometry of cloud,
the lonesome bird, the dark moon—

the dark moon shadowing a small world
of unsaid words, of tongueless wonder
where you like Alice wandered nameless,
forgetting quite who you meant to be,

desperate for lust to linger:
another motive for metaphor, stealing from
the weight of the ocean,
the fine bone of being,

the animal indifference, the anvil,
white and blue, the hot shock—
of tooth against suggestion—gunpowder,
the necessary, elusive, deadly, dominant O.

COME FROM AWAY

View of a Cat

(after Ted Hughes's *View of a Pig*)

The cat lay in a snowbank dead.
Its stiff weight seemed too heavy to lift.
Its eyes opened, blue and frozen.
Its tongue stuck straight out.

Its fur thick white spikes.
Cold in death seemed not quite dead.
Its warmth fled, further off.
It was like a bag of flour

I kicked without feeling guilty.
Children feel guilty kicking the living
and getting caught. But this cat
was not able to hiss or scratch.

It was too cold. Just too much
a mass of hair and bone.
Its last mystery had entirely gone.
It was not now a thing of fun.

Too dead now to wonder.
To remember its life, litter, lair
of human comfort as it had been.
Seemed unfair, beside the point.

Too deadly real, its weight
impressed me—how could it be moved?
And the trouble of warming it up!
The stare in its eyes was fierce but not menacing.

Once I ran up the stairs in the house
to catch a quick kitten
that was faster and nimbler than me,
its mewl was the wet sound of need.

This cat must have ice blood, it felt like a cold brick.
Its bite was worse than a dog's—
it snatched a half-moon clean out.
It ate sparrows, dead rats.

Distant admiration for predators such
as this was long over with.
I stared at it for a long time.
I was going to burn it.

Burn it and warm it back to breath.

Come From Away

*

Up the cliff the ring road dense
with cloudberries, bay a shit-filled
blue below, humpbacks, immense,

lost, bucking the chilled
flow, toss spume out to shore.
Most men pulp and paper mill

cast-offs, each season braced for
more lay-offs, pogey all through winter.
If you stay where you're

at, they'll come where you're to,
steady exodus to the mainland.
Radio news is who screwed who,

sermons, surgeries, deaths and
weddings. Oil drums squat hillside
like mushrooms and every man

Jack of ye prays for work, tide
to turn. Uptown the Walmart perches
unblinking, dropped like a time

machine to dwarf the shrinking churches,
All Saint's, Saint Mary's, Sacred Heart.
Feet swinging a ring over the dark earth,

a teenage boy was found, right smart
he was wound, swinging from a birch tree
over the jogger's trail. A sin, broke heart

his poor mother was. This town empties slowly,
water draining out of a tub, like molasses, dirty.

*

Being come from away since birth and without
a place to hide, you climbed into the kitchen cupboards,
burrowed into the flour sacks. Trout

silvered stinking in the sink, slippered women
shuffled over the shifting linoleum, taking up
jigg's dinner, Tupperware tumbling. The men

back from the offshore rig ready for a mug up,
rattling shotgun shells in your small palm, bloody
rabbits swung skinless from the line, chipped cup

tipped, hot teabag scorched your hand. "Sa skinny
I can sees the sin on yer soul. Get out me sight
fore I gives ye a crack so hard there won't be

enough of ye to pray over." Naked light
bulbs swung on frayed wire, scratch of cold
Hudson's Bay blanket you huddled in night

after night, sent to the bed of a lonely old
uncle, the hard stink of a chapped hand over
your mouth. Daylight, you, your uncle rolled

on the unhoovered carpet, he'd tickle, pester
until you cried. "Stop the youngster screechin',
she got me right drove." The German shepherd

kept outside strained against its chain, reaching
for the pan of dirty water it was your job to fill.
When you refused to pray, the minister, preaching

stricter measures, sharp tongued: "God's will
the youngster learns her lesson." Having taught
yourself to read you recited the alphabet until

you disappeared. Watched TV until you forgot
events you couldn't comprehend. In your dreams
your body dissected by a faceless monster, caught

in place, unable to defend yourself, scream.
When you told, retaliation followed. Dead kittens
face up in the toilet, dog left hungry, hot steam

scalded your skin. "G'wan, I was only makin'
out, bye. Ya got more lip than a coal bucket."
At the marina chancing frigid rapids, cracking

fat backs of mussels dying underfoot. Lax net
spilt seaweed ropes, you toed slimy balloons
of dead jellyfish over shore. Bellyache, threat

kept you outside checking traps, missing cartoons.
Monarchs carpeted the quarry. Hefted the dead
weight of antlers with both hands, afternoons

spent hot cheeked in snow plucking the heads
of small blue flowers. Forget-me-nots, you later
learned. Home like a blood knot twisted, petted,

and punished. "You some stunned, little frigger,
jinker. Where's your mudder to, mainlander?"

*

Three hours out of Port aux Basques
I am already sick for the city, unable
to upchuck into the Atlantic's flat glass

featureless weight of grey. The fable
of roaming moose recited on the straight
shot of the Trans-Canada Highway, bull

shit of course, doubt innate, lying
a hereditary trait. Speed by Bluebottom Pond,
a name you might equate

with still beauty but it's a campground
that stinks of shit, piss, empties rattle
underfoot. June snow coats Marble Mountain

where I have never slid, skied, fell
down white shafts ending in spin out.
Chairlifts ferry bright-cheeked clientele

to the apex in a ceaseless loop. Burnt out
bogs, charcoal trees ratcheting like skinny
antennae from ash, unkindness of ravens scouts

sky in search of intruders. Slate slant cranny,
slip past the Man in the Mountain, face picked
from random assemblage of rock, scrapepenny

Poppy says he guards gold in the river. Tricked
habitually, old scars itch. Truth's as shifting
as logjams in the Humber, best not to contradict.

Miles slide by under the wheel, what's drifting
past is constant, unchanged island, same graves,
memorials, steeples, same thick stench lifting

over town from the Mill. Instructed to behave
immediately upon arrival in Curling, a sloped
curve ending in clapboard houses and the nave

of All Saints. "Mind your mouth now." Groped
before I unpacked. "You is some nice piece
of stuff, my love, slack up." Weak rebuff I hoped

would suffice. "Dis rawny scut's Dougie's niece,
she be right miserable now bye, the first girl
to sleep in his bed," drunk Nan told the priest

at my uncle's wedding. "G'wan bye," heard
hissed through the tittering guests, ridicule
without rescue. "Mind now me son," hurled

at the groom. "Don't you be at dem fool
foxy heads now. Ya knows dere nuttin' but
spite cats." Relatives, half-cut, horny, pull

my red hair hard. Rare family portraits, smut
marred by hate. I guard against prayer, low tide
scavenge flotsam for treasure. Arrange my exit,

the Rock in reverse, dead porpoises in drift ice. They lied.
I've been come from away since birth. Nowhere to hide.

Grandfather

The flowers don't lie, I'm glad you finally
died; now we can snatch what you snuffed
of the light. Your pride another name for cruelty,

old man. A mismatch, you and the world, tough
love and a hard hand. Flushed blind kittens down
the toilet to whirl, drown. For spite you cuffed

the dog, your wife. When you got the girls alone,
overpowered any squirming, pillow on the face,
feet, hands bound. Shoved on the stairs, thrown

from the bed of the truck to a ditch. No place
was safe from your reach. Hurled scalding water
over the skin of your daughters. Erratic, chased

the littlest ones until, frantic, they fled to a mother
who refused to defend them. Struck so many times
she was too brittle, used to pretending slaughter

was cause for laughter. You favoured the crimes
of your son, praised for his prowess in theft, fights.
When drunk you sang your own nursery rhymes,

bounced the baby until his neck felt soft. Nights
you raced the truck up the ring-road, wheels hung,
spun, over the black water below, a fatal height

everyone prayed you would fall from. Hateful tongue
pointed to neighbours, pastor, sisters; to all
who dared reply. When I was four I was swung

like a doll over starboard, spray soaked my small
body, left me limp, phobic. Sick at the sight
of the sea. Too stunned to leave, they stayed loyal,

your children, your wife. You were hated, tyrant,
the rotted root of a twisted tree. You kept captive
a generation, wasted lives. Freed, tired, scant

time left to who survived you. But they're adaptive,
years of sorrow made them strong. They'll live.

My Son at Seven

When you were born there was no sound of celebration. Just a slick
slither as the doctor catches your wet body before it hits the floor.
The Red Sea pouring out of me, drowning you before you have the trick
of breathing—no cry, but a silence that deafens me with pitiless force.

Pregnancy was a lonely country, and your father, he was a battlement,
unmoved by me or you, growing fiercely inside. He is the blank space
in your baby pictures, the long shadow, the dark door, the entanglement
of bruises on my swollen body. He is the underpainting of your face.

At seven you were a dark colt, at nine you are a wolf, skirting the edge
of the playground. There are black things you have seen, half-moons
beneath your eyes. Near your head I hear planets wheeling, feel the ledge
of earth fall away from my feet. I'm satellite to your sun, ship to your anchor.

We huddle under blankets while beasts prowl around the bed.
You were seven: "God is a tree with many branches," you said.

Mother of Extinction

"God is a tree with many branches," you said. I
was skeptical, but it was too late to excavate
that fossil. We're a glacial epoch, survived
by no next of kin. Born to adapt, mutate,
I am the necessary end result. Chance decided
I live without accident. God's a vestigial function,
like the remains of eyes in cave-dwelling blind
fish, wings in flightless birds, hip bones
in whales and snakes. It's not an unusual event,
species regularly appear and disappear. Creation,
through loss and destruction becomes non-extant.
The lines of descent in our case a deformation
we won't speak of. Until you're willing to exhume,
you're the elephant in the middle of the room.

The Zoo

You're the elephant in the middle of the room.
One hundred and seventy pounds of ferocious meat
stalking my body, your child heavy in my womb,
kicking me from the inside. "You want me to beat
you, don't you?" Twirling the gun around a bony
finger, cocking it with deadeye aim at my head.
Panther prowl, gorilla arms, reptilian eyes stony,
hair glossy like the wing of a crow. "Now spread
your legs, I like it best when it's dry." I've lost
the will to try to reason with your monkey mind.
I've become wily, sneaky, learned never to cross
you. But when your child is born he becomes mine.
He will walk upright, evolve, and never speak your name.
You're a fracture in the door—impossible to contain.

For a Half Brother

You're a fracture in the door—impossible to tame,
reduce from a state of native wildness, be useful,
subdued. No beating made you docile, ashamed.
Adverse to cribs, cages, leashes, locks, you pulled
our mother face first into fear. You made me witness
to attempted escapes, hostile manoeuvres. Dulled
by defeat our mother retreated. Circling the compass
points your toes swing over the winter ground. Full
credit due to social workers, group homes. Beasts
raised you, savage was all you knew how to be. Truth
is, you were unloved. No one was less surprised than me.
Strangers found, boxed, buried, and prayed over you.
You were fruit dropped from a stunted tree, an aberration.
When you were born there was no sound of celebration.

Iron Highway

From Bishop Falls to Corner Brook the last
scheduled run hauled its live freight to the end
of the line. Officially abandoned, silver junegrass
spread fast, seedheads enshrined the railroad bed.

Childhoods spent bending stolen pennies
under heavy wheels of the Bullet dismantled,
scrapped like CPR's return tickets for Chinese
survivors of construction, detonation. Scandal

spiked the railway from Sydney to Courtenay,
passage of funeral trains carrying important
remains; prime ministers' bribe fattened frames
packed like heavily draped freight, escorted

past designated mourning stations, dry-eyed
natives blockaded, awaiting relocation.
Terra Transport sliced through the hillside
behind the house in Curling, bifurcation

of home from unknown domain, unfurling
marked map, this side of the track claimed
by third-generation Stones, Pikes, Kings.
Open season on mainlanders, fair game

to the firmly settled. She learned to duck
fists of ballast lobbed like black summer
snowballs at her face, but charcoal chunks
caught her hair, hammered from her

head to her Sunday-school dress, mess
earned her a wooden ruler across the back
of her thighs. After church, for redress,
surprised each bully with a blind attack,

stood above the rust of the flat ladder
she'd shoved them over, kicking patent
shoes into guts of distant cousins, mad her
punches couldn't murder. Mute combatant,

she let the distant whistle threaten, pinning
squirming prey beneath her knees, squeezing
soft throats to stifle screams, intent on wringing
submission from resistance, hold only easing

when choked pleas escaped blue lips, imminent
passage of the freight train vibrated the rails
and sleepers. Gripping the limp fists of impotent
enemies in her own, mimed lively hails

and waves at the locomotive's conductor, who
never failed to reply by pulling the cord
on the four-note steam trumpet, warning to
run from extreme danger, bell chime reward

to the child standing safely back from
the iron highway. They stayed away after
that, steered clear of the stranger dumped
on foreign family, someone's granddaughter

sent alone from Port aux Basques. Compelled
to sleep with her older uncle, wished whistle
code would work when the Bullet propelled
past the dark square of window glimpsed

over the stroking piston of the man above her.

The Minor Chord

The sadness will never end.
Daddy the drug dealer spoon-fed
my mother whatever candy she wanted,
LSD, amphetamine, when she was pregnant
with me. *Invisible hemangioma.*

After she gave birth to me, he forgot her
in the hospital waiting room. *It lives*
a quiet life, untouched by outside events,
hermit crab crouched in the rib cage.
Broke, she sat there for a day, me in her arms,

until a friend of a friend picked us up. *Black*
apple lodged in the throat. She was 21,
never had a shot at life. Her dad beat her
mom, all the kids were molested. *Where blood*
should be it runs humming, cresting white noise,

last train whistle. Everyone poor, no one
schooled. *Minor chord that breaks the heart again.*
Again. I was born with something wrong, a little off.
Cynic or sucker, bored or enchanted, doesn't matter.
I got broken as a baby, brain in pieces.

What it wants is to eat little by little the light.
No one can put me back together. It's not
an everyone feels sad sad. *Starving won't kill it,*
cutting won't let it out. No pill or prayer or poem
will shave it from the bone it cleaves to.

It's a constant, despair. *Elemental.*
Secret underside of a sparrow's wing,
deep dark of an unlit street in December.
The sadness will never end. *It will outlive*
us, its purity rare, untainted by desire

or even death. She was like that
my whole life. As long as I can remember,
just—dead eyes.
Cold hands. I was born like this.

Defective, unlovable, bad biology.
Sorrow inherited, unstoppable music
of the mitochondria. Relentless.
Innate, invincible. Ruthless.
Endless.

Tornado Chaser

My son scans the sky for supercell storms
the way I once watched ladders of light for signs
of the Rapture. He waits for squall lines to form,
cumulonimbus clouds to grow, decay, violent
twists of air to tear the earth apart. He wants to
capture wall clouds on camera, chase tornadoes
like a small child tied to a kite, see sliced-through
schools, demolished malls, levelled libraries. Rows
of stamped flat bungalows, tipped over telephone
poles. Attracted to the aftermath, debris delights
him like birthdays once did, enchanted by blown-
out windows, extinguished cities. Instability excites,
carnage charms. I lived in terror of sudden skyjack, driven
to Heaven. Accident's child loves fact, needs nothing forgiven.

Demasduit, 1819

For the month I was taken, they gave me the name
March, could also mean procession of People. Mary
for their mother. My own captured, murdered. Aimed
to release me without language, contaminated, carry
contagion home. Stole from my tongue two hundred
words, gave me a mouth full of noise. For his attempt
to protect me from them, six white men slaughtered
my husband. With a bough of truce on his forehead
they stabbed and left him dead on the ice. Loosed
from my arms our child, too, rots without wrappings
or careful cairn to hold his body in the earth, reduced
to carrion bare of odemet. Captive, they wring maps
from my blood, force me to sing, pray. I sickened, weak.
They called me Mary March. My name was Demasduit.

Shanawdithit, 1829

Her name was Demasduit; they called her Mary
March, as I am now Nancy; April, for the month
they brought me here. Sick with hunger, carried
from Badger Bay, sisters dead, father punched
a hole in the ice, died in water. For rescue men
are punished most severely, strength an affront
to the invader. For my salvation their children
are left in my care. Will never go home, among
intruders I die of the contamination that clings to
everything they occupy. They expect gratitude for
depredation, confused by refusal to be subdued,
assimilated. I tell them history, sketch the wars,
victories, births, deaths, stories. Hope they spare
land for those born here. Give them what's left,
piece of quartz, half-finished dress, lock of my hair.
They called me Nancy April. My name was Shanawdithit.

"—The tribe should hence be named 'Good Night Indians,'
Beothuck being the term for 'good night' in Mary March's
vocabulary. Indians generally have some other mode of
salutation than this; that word reads in the original
manuscript betheoate, evidently a form of the verb baetha:
to go home; and thus its real meaning is: 'I am going home'"

SYMPTOMS OF THE
DISORDER

Rate of Exchange

All attempts at empathy extinguished
during the exchange, dignity distinguished

from debasement by subtle rearrangement
of limbs, lips. Little lies force estrangement

of remorse from intent. Rupture material,
its urge, from mind. Greed eclipses initial

inhibition, blind need overtakes restraint,
apprehension of consequence, guilt's faint

reproach tossed aside for reprieve
the torso's weak defeat provides.

Deposition

She met his jerky gestures with alarm.
The truth is she's debris, heir
to a history of grim habitual harm,
mind unhitched, beyond repair.

The truth is she's debris, heir
to a curse of cruelty, misuse. Hostile,
mind unhitched, beyond repair,
trusting the sneer she mistook for smile.

A curse of cruelty, misuse, hostile
forces overtook her body as she choked,
trusting the sneer she mistook for smile,
sure nobody is punished unless provoked.

Forces overtook her body. As she choked
she met his jerky gestures with alarm,
sure nobody is punished unless provoked
by a history of grim habitual harm.

Testimony

He never meant to do her any harm.
This is the lie he will tell himself, swear
to all witnesses, she refused his charm,
so puzzled, he proceeded, unaware.

This is the lie he will tell himself, swear
aloud a chain of curses, manic, hostile,
so puzzled, he proceeded, unaware,
gagging the rictus he mistook for smile.

Aloud, a chain of curses, manic, hostile,
spit frenzied from his face as he choked,
gagging the rictus he mistook for smile,
dragging her slick weight, bloody, soaked,

spit frenzied from his face as he choked.
He never meant to do her any harm.
Dragging her slick weight. Bloody. Soaked.
To all witnesses: she refused his charm.

Portrait, Madrigal

Light unlocks her face, silk hair shed,
snarled in tendrils, a fist the night closed
opens, cups morning like a mystery exposed.

Debt of day, its need, spreads across the bed,
the upward tug, its greed for unopposed
light. Unlocks her face, silk hair shed,
snarled a tendrilled fist. The night closed

like a fist, locking its greed, tug. Dread
need to block any debt of love; opposed
to its smug spread, she keeps herself enclosed.
Morning opens upward, snarled light shed,
hair a fist of silk tendrils. Mystery, exposed,
cups her face like a lock the night closed.

Landscape, Madrigal

Light slices the bridge, rust-thick river
severs the valley, rigid geography shifts
in the shafts, surrenders its systems, lifts

what's left of its geology sunward. Sliver
of green cuts deft slits, topography adrift.
Light slices the bridge rust, thick river
severs the valley, rigid geography shifts.

Frigid wind shear hovers, truss, trestle quiver,
steel stringer sways in uncertain current. Swift
give in the updraft frees chaparral rooted in rift,
alight, it slices the bridge, thrusts quick upriver,
severs the valley. Rigid geography shifts
in the shafts, surrenders its systems, lifts.

Freight of Depression
(found)

A fever chart speaks with force
to the theorist, the therapist, the sufferer
and to all those who seek knowledge concerning

the dynamic of the psyche
the architecture of syntax
the intelligence of metaphor

betrayal is always reciprocal: the suicide betrays
the body, the ill person betrays love; but the speaker
herself has been betrayed by her beloveds
and by life itself

abandoned by mother,
father, husband, lovers
even sometimes daughters
who reject or hate or seduce her or die.

She is always responsible—
for wanting and needing too much,
for losing her balance,
for loving insufficiently,
for being born female.
For being born at all.

The punishment for guilt such as this is death.

Losses are multiple and crucial
integration is as often experienced
as disintegration
the self fused to the point of origin
does not always survive
the transition. Transformation
always entails the threat
of loss.

Because we do not know what madness is
and have never known
each historical moment
defines the boundaries differently
with a lack of certainty
but equally dogmatic conviction.
She served as ritual witness
to the inner lives.

Sporadically, a rhyme enters,
but it too carries the freight of depression:
everything is the same.

Nothing changes.

Symptoms of the Disorder
(found)

recurrent re-experiencing of the
(for example, troublesome memories, flashbacks
caused by reminders of the   recurring nightmares about
          and/or dissociative reliving of the   ),
avoidance to the point of having a phobia of places, people,
experiences that remind the sufferer of the   .
A general numbing
of emotional responsiveness, chronic physical signs
of hyperarousal, sleep problems, trouble concentrating, irritability,
anger, poor concentration, blackouts or difficulty
                                        remembering things,
increased tendency to be startled.

Hypervigilance to threat.

A lack of interest in activities that used to be enjoyed,
emotional deadness, distancing oneself from people, and/or
a sense of a foreshortened future.
                              must be present and must cause
significant distress or functional impairment
in order for the diagnosis to be assigned.

Explosive anger, passive aggressive behaviours; a tendency to forget
the   or feel detached from one's life or body,
persistent feelings of
shame, guilt or being completely different from others;

feeling the perpetrator of   is all-powerful
and preoccupation with either revenge against or allegiance with
the offender.
Severe change in those things that give the sufferer meaning,
like a loss of faith or
an ongoing sense of
helplessness, hopelessness,
or despair.

Tardive Dyskinesia

They have their own sweaty attraction,
bluntness of speech, fug of the
(*symptom*) unwashed
full of tremor (*side effect*).

This one (*symptom*) naked in snow,
points the pistol of his fingers to his temple
blows out the hidden sickness.
Born sane it's a gradual ascension;

should they love and in loving
make a nurse of the beloved?
(*symptom*) Heavy clothes in hot weather,
unbearable sadness (*side effect*).

Cruelty of cure, tardy disorder
occurs long after diagnosis,
result of lengthy treatment by medicine
(*side effect*) characterized by repetitive,

involuntary, purposeless movements:
(*side effect*) typing, sweeping, embracing,
weeping. Features of the disorder may include:
(*side effect*) smiling, speaking, inability to perceive

depth or its dangers. May be present:
grimacing, tongue protrusion,
lip smacking, puckering, pursing.
Grim facsimile of kiss.

Rapid movements of the arms, legs,
trunk may also occur. (*side effect*)
Involuntary movements of fingers
may appear as though the patient plays

an invisible piano. Tilts toward
unseen music, agrees with imperceptible
advisors, (*symptom*), wars with flutter
in the blood. Watches as you

(*symptom*) suddenly dance
to the patient's silent music,
point the pistol of your fingers
to your temple to still the music,

the movement, unceasing hunger,
(*side effect*) distress, rawness of skin.
Blow out the hidden sickness, traitor tongue,
kill all the ways our chemicals betray us.

Dyscalculia

(found)

Accelerated language acquisition: poetic ability.
Good visual memory for the printed word, areas of science
(until a level requiring higher math skills is reached),
geometry (figures with logic not formulas)

difficulty with the abstract concepts of time
and direction. Inability to recall sequences of past
or future events. Unable to keep track of time.
Mistaken recollection of names, poor name/face retrieval.

May be chronically late.

Inconsistent results in addition, subtraction, multiplication
            and division.
Poor mental math ability. Poor with money, credit, cannot budget.
Checkbooks not balanced. Fails to see big financial picture.
            May have fear
of money, cash transactions. Unable to mentally figure.

May be unable to comprehend or picture mechanical processes,
poor ability to "visualize or picture" the location of numbers
on the face of a clock, the geographical locations of countries,
oceans, streets. Poor memory for the layout of things.

Gets lost or disoriented easily.

number blindness

Inability to grasp and remember concepts, rules, formulas, sequence
(order of operations). Poor long-term memory
      (retention & retrieval)
of concept mastery—may be able to perform math operations
      one day,
but draw a blank the next

Blind Bluff

> *"Then wedge it by the thickness of the book*
> *that everything might keep the blackedged look*
> *of things, and that there might be time enough*
> *to die in, dark to read by, distance to love."*
> —*The White Lie*, Don Paterson

Doors close without escape
hatches opening elsewhere, doubt
a persistent tenant that checks, rechecks
locks, lights, the on and off,
blocks out the possibility of night
and its inhabitants. Tradeoff shook
from the tangle of ordinary terror,
bargain struck with self: stay sane.
Reclaim the remnants that he took
then wedge it by the thickness of the book

that a sliver in the sickness remains
unblocked. Shock delivers pain
along the network of the body in fits,
sparks, a radiance to infiltrate
the savage dark. She is a shoddy
reconstruction of life pre-left hook,
the hit that permits sleep and a license
to disembody. Sunlight, enemy of
the unloved, persists to both illuminate and spook
that everything might keep the blackedged look

the farthest corners of her treacherous
rooms. Even the table, sink, lecherous
with unstable stink, the taunting toilet
hole puke spattered, bile running up the
walls, plunking in chunks from the curtains,
rippled books, tuneless radio; traitorous stuff.
And the bed, crippled, sunk, surely swarming
with contagion. After, she felt the dumb love
of things, and that there might be time enough

to recover the safety of objects. Subterfuge
to self is senseless, heavy doses of vermifuge
crucial to purge the parasite that sits and nibbles
at the bastion of the brain. Best to abandon home
and body, head for internal turf. Tiresome to
assemble new asylum, but without
blueprints she breaks ground, there in the
interior where fear, the endless ache,
gives itself to her that there be grief enough
to die in, dark to read by, distance to love.

Take Back the Night
(found)

I. Small Note
Democratic Republic of Congo

Today by grace I take this small occasion
to tell you my history, my current situation.
In this small note I inform you that while
I worked in the fields with my hands, pulling
food from the earth for my brothers,
fathers, uncles, the Interahamwe
came to rape me. After, they took me
to the forest. I stayed there for three months.
After suffering mistreatment, I escaped
by foot to the hospital. I received medication
for six months and then gave birth to a
male child. He responds to the name Christophe.
Right now he is one year and three months old.
I study at the Institute, am in the first grade
of secondary school. In the first exam
I received a satisfactory grade of 60%.
Until now, I have not seen my parents.
I was born in Minova Gome in 1995.
In the moments when I remember the act
that the Interhamwe inflicted upon me,
truly, it breaks my heart.
Thank you. Greetings to you.
And to your family.

II. Valentine's Day

Canada

My story will seem small in comparison
but between the ages of 8 and 12 I was
sexually assaulted by my cousin. I am now 13.
The worst part was that when it wasn't
happening I almost wished it was.
I felt used, unloved. I know there are other
people like me but I wish I were all alone.
Then no one would have to feel the pain
that I have felt and feel. The first person I told
was Sherry. Then I told Marilyn, then Alison.
They told me to tell the school counselor.
She told the school principal. She told me to tell my parents.
On Valentine's Day, I told them what he did.
They said: "You don't have to speak to him
or be alone with him again. Don't think too much about it.
He probably didn't know what he was doing."
What they will never accept is that he did.
He ruined my life; I'm pretty sure I can't let it go.
I will never forgive him. I'm not ready. Yet.
This part of my life is over and done.
I just hope that no one will ever have to experience
what I went through ever again. But the world isn't perfect.
I try to remember that no matter how many bad people
there may seem to be on this planet,
there are always more good ones.
I haven't started dating but I like a really nice
guy in my math class. I hope he likes me, too.

III. The Garden

India

I do not like to recollect it, ever, what happened to me,
3 years ago in Assam in the large garden behind the house
with my cousin. He was having difficulties, he said,
with his girlfriend. He wanted to tell me about this.
But today I know, this was a lie. As soon as we were far
from the house he grabbed me, when I screamed, he hit me.
In my puzzled state, I was restrained from screaming further.
Before I knew, through a multitude of pain, I was raped.
Once he finished, out of my trauma, I could not move
although I was in my senses.
Facing no disturbances or resistances
he raped me over and over again.
People found me in a pool of blood at dusk.
By then, I was senseless.
My aunt, his mother, is so influential in the family.
Everybody knows that my cousin, is a remarkable boy.
Nobody believed me.
They never listen to women.
I was seventeen then.
I shall never be seventeen again.

IV. Swimsuit

United Kingdom

When I was nine, Mum had a breakdown
after Grandma died. My brothers and I were
sent to live with my drug addict dad;
he brought his friends home to crash.
One night my father went out with his friends
leaving a man behind to look after us.
Since my mum went away I couldn't sleep.
I'd lie awake listening to Dad and his friends
talking all night long.
This night was different.
My brothers were asleep, everything was silent.
I heard him enter my room.
I faked I was asleep, hoping he'd go away.
At that age I already knew what was going to happen to me.

He crawled on the bed, lay next to me.
I didn't move, didn't know what to do as he started
to touch me. He pulled aside my undies and went inside me.
I was freaked but I still pretended to be asleep.
He started to rub himself against my behind,
then quietly went out.
I stayed up all night, couldn't think what to do.
I had no one to turn to.
The next night I put on my full bodied
swimsuit to protect myself if he decided to do it again.

After my dad went out he came into my room
but this time left after a few minutes of rubbing
my privates because he couldn't get easy access.
The next night when my father planned to go out
I started crying, begged him not to go.
He looked at all his friends and smiled and said:
"See how much she cares for me."
He said he'd stay. He lied. He always lies.
That night his friend entered my room again
and this time he got what he wanted.
I just lay there like I was sleeping
as he pulled my panties off and spread my legs.
He found it hard to get inside, couldn't fit,
so he did something that at the time to me
was horrible, freaky. He went down on me,
spat and pushed his tongue inside of me.
I kept pretending to be asleep, keep my breathing even.
Then he tried to enter me again.
This time it worked a little as he slowly eased it in.
I tried to look like I couldn't feel anything.
Kept my eyes closed. Soon he was just shoving and shoving,
starting to really kill me, I thought, I will die.
I hit him with my hands, tried to push him off me,
scratched, started crying.
He pinned my wrists together and said:

"Shut up or I'll tell your dad what you did."
So I kept still. Played dead until he finished.
He came inside me, I know that now.
After he was done he cleaned himself up with
the swimsuit I had been too stupid to wear.
It was hanging from my bedpost.
It would have kept me safe.

V. Better Than My Mom

Australia

It's gonna feel weird I just know it.
He's pacing the floor right now.
I have been reading these stories.
I can relate to a lot of them.
He has no idea what I'm doing.
He's pouring his coffee but
in about ten minutes it'll happen again.
He says I'm better than my mom,
I'm the only one who can do it right.
I wish I was dead. I am sorry.

VI. The Pen is My Weapon
South Africa

My father took my virginity so hard when I was 7,
forced me to touch his private part, told me to put his thing
in my vagina. I bled so hard when he raped me, there was blood
all over my hands, legs, clothes. He promised to kill me if I told.
When I was 12, a man used to stop me from going to school,
undress me without raping me, lick me all over my body
touch my breasts very hard, put his hand in me.
When I was 15 I was gang raped by 10 men.
I can say that I was dead, numb.
They also put a candle in my private part, I couldn't
walk for a week. I didn't report it. My mum was not there,
she was a domestic worker, she didn't live with us.
I'm the only girl at home and last born. I
was raped again by 4 men when I was 16.
Again when I was 17 by 2 men.
It is really hard to let it go, and I can't.
Life is over now. I'm looking forward
to helping myself but it is so hard.
I was abused by my father almost every day, I couldn't
report him because he paid my school fees. I needed him to survive.
He did this for two years. One night I refused, tried to fight him.
He beat me up so badly, said I don't appreciate him.
I lost three teeth, woke up the next day with a swollen face.
In one year I had 4 miscarriages.
Regardless of the suffering I've been through

I am grateful that I am still alive to share my story with someone
who thinks she might be alone because
there were times I thought I was alone.
I'm tired of being a victim and being expected to survive.
I'm working on getting over it but I keep getting raped.
I'm tired of all the times a man feels it his right to grab
my butt or breast or any part of my body.
I'm so tired, the next bastard that puts their hand on me
will have a pen in his eye. This is a weapon
I never leave home without.
I'm sick of how the world made it a rule
that women shouldn't walk
around outside alone.
What freedom do we have when the truth
is we are restricted in movement.
All I've got to say is I'll die being me,
I'd rather die free than live in prison.

For the Left Behind

Straddling the lattice and struts of the viaduct, *our possible life*
dipping from dawn to day over the river. Backside of billboards,
dark playgrounds. *What could becomes what was.* Tilting Victorians
rot near overgrown vacant lots. Smashed flat corpses of pigeons

pancake the pavement. Burst black bags, beat down women.
What was left behind after the clean up, the razing. Rapacity
as forward thinking. Good planning. Particular about where
the garbage goes. Straddling smashed flat corpses of beat down

women, rapacity as rot. Overgrown playgrounds, pigeons,
vacant lots. *Possible life becomes what was.* Burst black bags,
backside of billboards. The garbage goes from dawn to day
over the river. Good planning. *What could was left behind*

after the clean up, the razing. Thinking women tilting forward.
Smashed flat Victorians, burst bags, lattice and struts of corpses
rot near dark playgrounds. *Our could becomes particular life.*
Dawn burst a black pancake over the river, dark pigeons

where the garbage goes. Overgrown women, left behind.
Forward over the viaduct rapacity *becomes what was our life.*

The November Revolution

Oppenheimer's Beach

To the people of St. John for public park and recreation
area, Toni, Trinity's granddaughter willed the remains
of a house succumbed to disaster, dark rubble patient
in collapse. Clearance refused, choice reduced, she became
Death, wrapped a rope around rafters, ligature as elegant
as any equation, wound remainder to rest upon her carotid
arteries. Suspended herself like heavy cloud, an event
without mystery, afterthought of fallout. Land allotted
by legacy left unattended, soon returned to its native state
of instability, adorned with graffiti, untroubled by tenants
or upkeep, rotted down to intrinsic parts. Ability to translate
departed her, descendent of the radiance of a thousand suns
bursting over White Sands, inherited megatons of splendour,
the might that pulled her body from the ceiling to the floor.

Coordinator of Rapid Rupture

*"As West and East / In all flatt Maps—and I am one
—are one, / So death doth touch the Resurrection."*

"Now we are all sons of bitches." Lighting
beggared description, whole country searing
with intensity many times that of the midday
sun. Gold, purple, violet, blue, and grey,
lit every peak, crevasse, and ridge of nearby
mountain range with a clarity and a beauty
that must be seen to be imagined. Hypocentre
of The Gadget's creation: Robert J. Oppenheimer,
Trinity's father, responsible for fast neutron
chain reactions, abnormal residual radiation,
slick crater of melted desert one thousand
feet wide. Bestowed contamination to span
six decades after detonation without sign
of cessation. Skinless survivors lined
up for mercurochrome treatments, crisp
corpses of four-year-olds, bodies drift
downriver, flood of the dead. He knew
after his first act, hosting summer school
for bomb theory, that the world would never
be the same. Along the roadside scattered
piles of scorched horses. Night at noon.
"There was nothing we could do."

Eyewitness Account of the Science Writer
(found)

WAR DEPARTMENT
PRESS BRANCH SUNDAY,
SEPTEMBER 9, 1945

On our way to bomb Japan,
a small group of scientists, Army, Navy representatives,
privileged to be present at the ritual of its loading,
a thing of beauty, this "Gadget," millions
of man-hours, brain-power focused on taming the Atom.
Only under certain conditions can it be made
to give up the greatest explosion on earth.

The midnight briefing ended with a moving prayer by the Chaplain.

In command of our mission Major Charles W. Sweeney, 25.
His flagship "The Great Artiste" carrying the bomb.
An hour away from base the storm broke.
Eerie light above the Navigator's cabin,
whirling propellers become luminous discs of blue flame,
the windows, nose of ship, tips of wings, riding fire.
One's thoughts dwelt anxiously on the precious cargo
in the invisible ship ahead of us.

Sergeant Curry, who had been listening steadily,
busied himself decoding a message from outer space,
"Think this will end the war?"

"There is a good chance this one may do the trick.
But if not the next one or two surely will."

Ocean, sky, merge into one great sphere.
Inside of that firmament, riding mountains of clouds,
suspended in infinite space. Motors soon become
insignificant against the immensity all around
and are before long swallowed by it.
There comes a point where space also swallows time,
one lives through eternal moments filled with
oppressive loneliness, all life suddenly vanished
from the earth and you are the only one left,
a lone survivor traveling endlessly through space.

We rode out the storm on a direct line to the Empire.
Hours from now one of its cities, making war against us
will be wiped off the map by the greatest weapon
ever made. In one-tenth of a millionth of a second,
time immeasurable by any clock, a whirlwind
from the skies will pulverize
thousands of its buildings,
tens of thousands of its inhabitants.
Does one feel pity for the poor devils about to die?
Not when one thinks of Pearl Harbor.
The death march on Bataan.

The winds favor certain Japanese cities that remain
nameless. We circled about them again, again, found

no opening in the thick umbrella of clouds.
Destiny chose. Out of the belly of the Artiste
a black object came down, great flash broke
the dark barrier, flooded our cabin with intense light
that lingered, illuminated the sky.
Blast wave struck our ship, tremble from nose to tail,
like the boom of cannon hitting from all directions.
Observers on our ship saw

a giant ball of fire rise from the bowels of the earth,
belching forth enormous white smoke rings.
45 seconds had passed.
A pillar of purple fire, 10,000 feet high, shooting skyward
a meteor coming from earth instead of space, ever more alive
as it climbed through clouds. No longer smoke, dust, or even fire.
A living thing, a new species of being, born right before our eyes.
At one stage of its evolution, covering missions of years
in seconds, the entity assumed the form of a totem pole,
its base three miles long, tapering off to a mile at the top.
Bottom brown, center amber, top white, carved with many
grotesque masks grimacing at the earth.

When it appeared settled into state of permanence,
came shooting out of the top a giant mushroom,
increased the height of the pillar to 45,000 feet.
Mushroom top more alive than pillar, seething
in a fury of foam, sizzling upwards, descending earthward,
a thousand Old Faithful geysers struggling in elemental fury,

breaking bonds that held it down. It freed itself from its
gigantic stem momentum carrying into the stratosphere
to a height of 60,000 feet.

No sooner did this happen when another mushroom,
smaller than the first, began emerging out of the pillar,
the decapitated monster growing a new head.
As the first mushroom floated off into the blue
it changed its shape into a flower-like form, giant petal
curving downward, creamy white outside, rose-colored inside.

It still retained that shape when we last gazed at it

                                    from a distance of 200 miles.

The Heavy Hearts of Atoms

Like all objects, you persist. Heavy matter
pinioned to an elementary Earth, gravity
engraving its weight upon your brow.
Water brought to shore, current's cold velocity,

crustacean's silent trawl; without this,
the essential composition of it all would be
radically strange. Stars would shine differently.
You would not exist. You are a sequence,

part of a fundamental force, and all of it,
memory, action, love, betrayal, is nothing
but the charges of the heavy hearts of atoms.
Symmetry breaks, but one does not know

in which direction. You are a cloud of electrons
circling without centre. Yet you insist somewhere,
someone has an answer to the elusive question.
Someone, somewhere, will pick up the phone

when you call in the night. Somebody understands.
Someplace, they wait for you, the door unlocked.
You are just a relationship between particles and the forces
of the universe. But mathematically, you are beautiful.

Of Grace Attempted

Blastocyst like a barnacle resisting
expulsion. Stubborn freight scraped
into wet pieces, a bloody propulsion.

Incomplete structures subjected
to stresses, oscillations that would
not arise after completion. Construction

is potentially a grave hindrance
to existing traffic and normal life.
Above ground, until spans are joined,

wind can be a great hazard.
Some form of bracing will often be required.
Some semblance of grace attempted.

Nothing is spared, tolerated, or illuminated.
Cold molecular clouds collapse under
their own weight, fragment into pieces.

M-Theory

In which you enter something new
and so, you hope, better. Symmetry splits
potential into endless variants; you

swing from one situation to the next,
ape in search of higher ground, mate.
Thin strings, single signals, permit

everything: worlds, waves, weight
of your intentioned decisions allow
for life, collection of events that fluctuate

with each choice. Define your tomorrows
with gravity, how an hour's soft substance
presses on the cavity of your chest, slows

blood and time. The voice of chance
lures with the illusion of luck, greater
fortune. Somewhere in the expanse

of the furrowed folds of matter,
you make the right decision; light, love,
shelter follow. Elsewhere, mistake or

accident stays your twitchy hand, results of
which vary. Try again. Call the cosmic bluff.

Cantilever

What was wrought rusts,
buckles under bright buttresses.

Sleeplessness the cause of structural
deficiencies, repetitive stresses,

eventual decline. Torsion distorts,
diffracts light, objects resonate

from related frequencies, external forces.
Extract harmonic motion, oscillation

wave energy leaking through holes,
propagating as if centres were sources,

congregating spherically, steadily, particles
seep, separate, instability spreads wreckage

of immense amplitudes. Being weak, fickle,
rocks the caisson, shocks status. Gauge

unreliable indicator of insecurity, powerless
to resist compulsions that cause material

deformation
        structural collapse

Uncertainty Principle

Uncertainty is a quirk of the world, primary
property of truth. We are all interconnected
by laws, a woman subject to the same authority
as a quasar, a man adherent to the perfected
model of mitochondria. But history shifts,
inconstant, dysphoria follows love without
a known outcome, imprecise limits, drifts
into states of "neither-nor," door of doubt
opens where the usual facts of existence
break down. We have no way to determine
eventual decay, no states of definite
position, momentum. Just a prescription
to calculate observer interference, default
decoherence, divorce—all possible results.

Spooky Action at a Distance

spukhafte Fernwirkung

He's her hypothetical counterpart, mirror twin
to her ordinary matter, scattershot amount
of his particles coheres thinly to her skin,
carrying a constant charge she can't account
for without calculating large failings, flaws.
Theoretically, he exists, but his absence
outweighs his actuality. Useless to pause
factuality's malaise. Can't afford consequence
of a break with parity. She knows eventually
their elements will, after urgent interaction,
be separated by indifferent entropy.
Absolute entanglement, acute attraction,
will decohere, irreversibly. Uncouple from each
other in limitless loss, unbearable breach.

Dopplengänger

Peripherally, you glimpse yourself in other lives, sinister
in the way you lounge against a bus stop, scrounge for change,
appear to wait for someone to arrive. A variant you administers
sterile sentiment to the simple and trusting. Solicit exchange,
you for them, trade careers, spouses, situations. Your misery
for their agony. Pretend you will be happy, alternate as upgrade,
that a difference in story will supplant the traps you've laid, free
you from the ordinary order that you cling to, conclusions you evade.
As though your double, duped into your delusion will not then ask
"How long do you mean to be content?" Then set about the ruin
of your life, levelling careful props, proof that you belong, massed
objects you've collected. Fearful upheaval will prove your undoing,
display you, unprotected. Pray the duplicate, its trick undetected,
will be more merciful than you. Conceal the obverse, leave you perfected.

The Corruption of Charm

During the November Revolution you were found
whirring below baryons, both Lilliputian and leviathan,
principal player in the fundamental floor show. Unbound,
you ruin our rules, flaunt our fascination, fixation
with your come-hither temptation. We want you secure,
settled, unaltered by the invasion of our eyes. Stripped
of your mystery, your function's necessity assured.
We want to be right. Certain calculations, equipped
to uncover how you will behave when force is applied.
Tease out your flavour, strangeness, source of weakness.
Prove our expertise in dissection. Allay what we can't abide;
at close range, coherence decays. Equations cheat, guess
at detection. Fret the wretched compression, our timeline
finite, quick. Transfixed by the trick of your mean lifetime.

Beauty, Banged

Decayed up, you're charming, though byproduct
of the big boson and not on your own very lovely;
dumpy, disarming. We plot lethal collisions, conduct
shady studies, squeeze sweet secrets from your shy
sashay. Many millions of you nullified, the complex
patterns of your death will show us what is not.
Plump assumptions, the case of missing matter, vex
us. Like detectives we detest what perplexes, hot
for the striptease, the peel that reveals the supreme
perfection of our cleverest premise. Unzip and bang,
wreckage leaves clues, suspects, evidence at the scene.
Reconstruct the crime, replay the picosecond we sprang
improbably, orphaned, out of the fray. Lonely, we violate your parity,
validate theory. Grateful to annihilate your fleeting radiance, its rarity.

Dark Matter

The systems of your body are mostly
dark matter, undetectable but inferred
by the grief you carry, heavy, costly,

your quarks fatter with its incurred
freight. In your centre sits a daemon,
an elementary black hole undeterred

by your desire. Gravity's radiation
a weight that keeps you bed-bound,
requires your best impersonation

of you, before. Ignore the unsound
advice of professionals, your missing
mass evidence of Magellanic Clouds

clustered in confines of your persisting
person. Thrust hard from inertia, take
loss into calculations. Preexisting

conditions exacerbated by a break
from parity, mirrored particulate
circulating with temerity in the wake

of collapse. Anatomy's temporary state
a flux of rest and combat, neutron bomb
both unassailable and frail, poised to detonate.

DIMINISHING RETURNS

Signal Light on the Horizon

Some nights, we chase sleep across
the earth, a swift tilt slippery beneath
our feet, racing against fixed defeat
and the clenched fist fall, stockpiling loss
to forestall the inevitable. Tally the cost
of the small crimes; glances, blood heat,
innuendo weighed against our conceit.
We chance diminishing merit to the dross
moments of possible. It doesn't signify,
our actions before the event. Sometimes
there is unrelated catastrophe, signal light
on the horizon, without a warning cry
to go below. We lie. Awake, dreading time
in the half-empty bed. Moth-eaten nights.

Pantheon

The half-empty bed, moth-eaten nights, nothing so
beautiful as the sharp relief of shadows on the school
walls, boy in a leather jacket waiting under the trees below.
Forget what you know about hunger or being cruel.
Be fifteen, restlessness driving you out the window
into the summer dark down the drainpipe, surviving
the short fall but not that boy or the ones who
came later. Memory will render them gods taking
places in your essential mythos, your internal pantheon.
Forget what you learned about sex. Be fucked against
the playground fence. You haven't felt that in an eon.
Possibility was fishnet tights and a bus pass. Condense
longing down to a singular story. Sleeplessness the cost.
Dawn a distant country. So a woman will hold loss.

Entropy

Dawn a distant country, so a woman will hold loss
tightly as ballast, the question mark of her
belly deflated. Light sinks in the chinks, the cost
of living alone. Runagate, transience a regular
state. Plans sprout and slacken, occur
naturally, unaided. We progress without volition
toward eventual demolition. What we prefer
is incidental, biology runs itself without hesitation,
intervention, or prayer. Occasional pain a perforation
in the lie we've all agreed to. Awareness of the lack,
her empty topography breeds a dry despair,
frees the future from the yoke of need. Track
hours around the clock, clasp absence dear and slight
to her breasts tenderly. Now turn her face from light.

Infection

Turn her face from light and choke
out the need to breathe. Your contagion
replaces the vital system, substitution
for rights or release. When she spoke
there was only clamour, din. You broke
her final resistance, demanding oblivion,
scouring away identity. She—an obstruction
to fulfilment, to the fixed intent to evoke
curse and transcendence. A shrill dent
that worsens as the oxygen leaks out.
Fear's a cheap hallucinogen worth
the cost of capture and tears. You spent
years unmooring this moment. Fallout
fixing her forever anchored to the earth.

Flummox the Watchers

Other nights, anchored to the earth
we clutch at dark cloud. Resistance
to orbits of influence is futile. Purge
fragile from your vocabulary. Insistence
on equilibrium is laughable. Vertigo
a natural reaction under the circumstance
and the only side effect allowed. Show
some moxie. Some pluck! Leave chance
to the schmucks. Flummox the watchers
of fate. Create, don't manifest. Bullshit's
capacious and contagious, answers
for any opposition to evolution. Submit to
nothing. Admit you've failed to extort
all peace or a sleep like a mother comforts.

Derailment

As a mother comforts we have navigated
this terrain—like an unfolded map hung
between us. Delicate manoeuvres phase
out most of the damage. Among
obstacles: hours, miles, families, far-flung
scatter of sentiment meted out in packets
by post. Lost letters matter more, unsung
lyrics limn the days' outline. Exit's hatchet
job the tacit admission to failure and forfeit.
Watchmen nix a union of the actual (airmail
a so-so substitute for the body's foiled attempt
to fornicate). Too late to curtail the full-scale
derailment. Over and done for, when we measure
our worth by the map of skin worn by another.

Bit Player

Navigated our worth by the map of skin
we're born with, yet still find the blank
expanse lacking. Worn whorls, sag. Frank
assessment spent pinching the fat. If thin
was booty it was stolen by your freak twin
during a neglect of duty, sent into dank,
dangling exile. Days when you were wank
material final. Never mind. Take it on the chin.
You were never fragile. Nobler to chicken out
than to mollycoddle dead dreams. All we said
about cream rising is shit. Don't begrudge
beauty that quickens the blood, don't doubt
your use. Bit player, middler, filler, living dead—
occupy a multitude of mornings, the commuter crush.

Postal

Mornings, the commuter crush annihilates
dregs of dream. Routine replacement
for actuality. Boring, boring: say it. Wait
for relief, die at your desk. Tormented
by pesky other-thans and shoulds. Lie when asked
about your goals, gains. As if this were one,
washing up on the shoals of deadlock, tasked
to campaign for your own redundancy. Guns
figure largely in your fantasies. The boss's brains,
blown out across the lips of cubicle walls, decorate
shaky stacks of to-dos. Urgent calls remain
unanswered. Eclipsed by your might, workmates
stagger upright and free, toss confetti, high fives.
As if. Across the platform, smeared faces, bleary eyes.

Promotion From Within

Smeared faces, bleary eyes, newspaper headlines
bind the morning in familiar arms. Bulldoze
the swarm of straphangers, go-getters. Define
distance by the days between letters. We chose
to resist resistance by aligning with the gross
forces of the rich and hungry, our early selves
placated by special deliveries. Boring to oppose
what we all know is the evil paradigm. Tell
it to someone with time to kill, it's a soft sell
to the already sold. Every inter-office envelope
brief relief snorted from toilet backs to quell
remnants of regret. Panic wells but we cope.
Our good works wouldn't have mattered much.
Bum a last cigarette before work's bleak rush.

Keep Unfixed

Before work's bleak rush you clung hard
to the weak crutch belief made. Gradual
decline in conditions eroded individual
inclinations. Brief excursions west marred
expectations of love, success. Disregard
dismissals, promotions. Fulfil contractual
obligations and move on. Try bisexual
for sticky, quick distraction. Guard
against complications, keep unfixed
affairs. Up is relative and could mean high.
Keep mobile. Do what it takes to prosper,
also relative and could mean debt. Xeroxed
résumés double as dating profiles. Comply
with what diminishes us from vigour to vapour.

Higgs Boson

Diminishes us. From vigour to vapour we decay,
half-life of an energetic body slowed, unwound.
You, elementary, give mass to material, weigh
our dark matter with invisible scales. Earthbound,
detectable details could disprove you were here.
We know you by your absence, smashed particles,
the mess you leave behind. Our best guess mere
conjecture. So a woman, lost, steers by your pull,
chance, all events occurring simultaneously: youth,
clumsy love, untruth, failure, loss. Choices the mercy
of uncertainty, frail props of reason. Unstable truth
collides with desire, constant probability debris
in her body. Exhaust theory; we cannot predict her place
or hours, dark wing-beats over the contours of her face.

Here In Delirium

Hours dark wing-beats over the contours
of her face, half-life of the hypersomniac
flickers, indistinct. Sleep's deep roots are scars
 in the skeleton, radiating fatigue crack
along the body's fault lines. Fear of flashback
keeps her slight, supine. Once there was
a morning that lasted years, vital attack
on all fronts, indefatigable—assault, pause,
onslaught, pause, obliterate. Withdraw
to Nod, hunch under the blanket's buffer,
take up residency in a land where the law
is just, in dream's country, assailants suffer
for their sins. Here in delirium she begins
to erase the sum of all choices, the origin.

Hidden Possible

We are the sum of all our choices, accidents,
and intent. Observe and effect collapse;
construct of our built life caves in, traps
us in its details. Rife with guilt, regrets, we invent
conditions, circumstance. When chance presents
an opening in the hours, work, firing of synapse,
don't shirk the fluke. Let space, infinite, unmap
your body. Hook faith on the seen, your misspent
rebuke of self, situation, useless freight. Sublimate
remorse, by the freefall timescale it's negligible,
as are you. Name the systems and embrace
delusion. You move from one equilibrium state
to another after sudden change, the hidden possible
all that hangs between illusion and the origin of grace.

Shits and Giggles

We're the origin of grace, dumb monkeys
dabbling in a too-big pond. Delinquents
 tinkering in the gluons and the bosons, disease
of curiosity specific to our species, malcontents
determined to pick apart the universe, like
combing lice from our fur. Unqualified, we
gleefully smash atoms, believe our own hype,
determine civilization by its proximity to coffee.
Ankle-biters trashing all we get our paws on. Ass
holes fucking with the fundamentals, frat boys
date-raping dark matter. Kicking the looking glass
for shits and giggles. We are background noise,
transmitting primitive signals to cold, vacant space,
spreading simian seed all over the nights we chase.

Diminishing Returns

Some nights, we chase sleep across
the half-empty bed. Moth-eaten nights,
dawn a distant country. So a woman will hold loss
to her breasts, tenderly, and turn her face from light.
Other nights, anchored to the earth
by someone else's body, sleep like a mother
comforts. We have navigated our worth
by the map of skin worn by another.
Mornings, the commuter crush,
smeared faces, bleary eyes. Newspaper,
coffee, last cigarette before work's bleak rush
diminishes us from vigour to vapour.
Hours dark wing-beats over the contours of her face.
We are the sum of all our choices, the origin of grace.

Roxanna Bennett was born in Toronto, Ontario but spent much of her childhood in Corner Brook, Newfoundland. She studied Experimental Arts at the Ontario College of Art and Design and Creative Writing at the University of Toronto. Currently she lives in Whitby, Ontario with her son and partner. *The Uncertainty Principle* is her first book.

Page 66 "Freight of Depression"
Diane Wood Middlebrook and Diana Hume George, introduction to *The Selected Poems of Anne Sexton*, by Anne Sexton, ed. Diane Wood Middlebrook and Diana Hume George (New York: First Mariner Books, 2000), xi-xxiii.

Page 68 "Symptoms of the Disorder"
"Posttraumatic Stress Disorder," MedicineNet, http://www.medicinenet.com/posttraumatic_stress_disorder/page4.htm.

Page 72 "Dyscalculia"
"Symptoms," The Dyscalculia Forum, http://www.dyscalculiaforum.com/viewpage.php?page_id=1.

Page 76 "Take Back the Night"
Sourced from anonymous posts on various online sexual assault forums. Names have been changed or deleted.

Page 91 "Eyewitness Account of the Science Writer"
William L. Laurence, "Eye Witness Account: Atomic Bomb Mission Over Nagasaki," War Department press release, September 9, 1945, quoted on AtomicArchive.com, http://www.atomicarchive.com/Docs/Hiroshima/Nagasaki.shtml.

ACKNOWLEDGEMENTS

I gratefully acknowledge the financial support of the Ontario Arts Council and the Writer's Reserve program in particular.

Thank you to my chosen family: Brian Skene, Chris Turner, Edward Barao, Steve Bevan, Felicity Hanlan, Lisa Villary, Kathryn Waugh, Lara Bazant, Kamlyn Ng-See-Quan, with deep gratitude to Donald 'O.M.' Sybilis for scaring me into doing this. Probably none of you will read this far to the back of the book to know your names are in it so HA HA and I love you.

Thanks to Cameron Clow for first draft suggestions.

Thank you to Jay Pitter, Sonja Greckol, Debra Bennett, Jarrah Hodge, Serena Freewomyn, who encouraged and inspired.

Thank you to the women who care for me: Angela Wong, Susie Costello, Erin Kuri, Amanda Drisdelle.

Super extra thanks to Tara-Michelle Ziniuk and Jon Paul Fiorentino for hand-holding.

Special thanks to Ken Babstock who said I could and should.

Thank you to the following journals whose editors first accepted these poems for publication, sometimes in slightly different forms:

"The Bottle Genie" in *RedZine*

"Break Up" in *Popshot*

"Flummox the Watchers," "Tornado Chaser," "Bit Player," in *Contemporary Verse 2*

"Signal Light On The Horizon" in *Slice Magazine*

"Symptoms of the Disorder" in *vallum: new international poetics*

"Gravity's Hook" in *The Toronto Quarterly*

"Dyscalculia" in *The Dalhousie Review*

"Diminishing Returns" (previously titled "Navigating Our Worth") in *Descant*

"My Son at Seven" in *Existere*

"Jeremy" in *The Malahat Review*

"So Long, Leonard" in *The Antigonish Review*

"Another Motive for Metaphor" in *The Fiddlehead*